OUTDOOR EXPLORERS

3 West

Helen Foster James

Published in the United States of America
by Cherry Lake Publishing
Ann Arbor, Michigan
www.cherrylakepublishing.com

Reading Adviser: Marla Conn MS, Ed., Literacy specialist, Read-Ability, Inc.

Photo Credits: © Jim David / Shutterstock.com, cover, 1; © XiXinXing / Shutterstock.com, 6; © Mamontova Yulia / Shutterstock.com, 8, 12; © Frank L Junior / Shutterstock.com, 10; ©Ian Grainger / Shutterstock.com, 10; © Geartooth Productions / Shutterstock.com, 11; © steve estvanik / Shutterstock.com , 11, 13; © sebastianosecondi / Shutterstock.com, 12; © fertatay / Shutterstock.com, 13; © Ethan Daniels / Shutterstock.com, 14, 19; © Warren Metcalf / Shutterstock.com, 16; © David Osborn / Shutterstock.com, 16; © Tom Reichner / Shutterstock.com, 17; © Harold House / Shutterstock.com, 17; © davidhoffmann photography / Shutterstock.com, 18; © blewulis / Shutterstock.com, 18; © Peter Moulton / Shutterstock.com, 19; ©oliveromg / Shutterstock.com, 20; © TravnikovStudio / Shutterstock.com, 20; © Yiorgos GR / Shutterstock.com, 20; © urbans / Shutterstock.com, 20; © Ben Harding / Shutterstock.com, 22; © Tom Olson / Shutterstock.com, 22; © The Adaptive / Shutterstock.com, 22; © James Marvin Phelps / Shutterstock.com, 22

Library of Congress Cataloging-in-Publication Data
Names: James, Helen Foster, 1951- author.
Title: West / Helen Foster James.
Description: Ann Arbor : Cherry Lake Publishing, 2017. | Series: Outdoor explorers | Includes bibliographical references and index. | Audience: Grades K to 3.
Identifiers: LCCN 2016057054| ISBN 9781634728782 (hardcover) | ISBN 9781634729673 (pdf) | ISBN 9781534100565 (pbk.) | ISBN 9781534101456 (hosted ebook)
Subjects: LCSH: Natural history—West (U.S.)—Juvenile literature.
Classification: LCC QH104.5.W4 J36 2017 | DDC 508.78—dc23
LC record available at https://lccn.loc.gov/2016057054

Cherry Lake Publishing would like to acknowledge the work of the Partnership for 21st Century Skills. Please visit www.p21.org for more information.

Printed in the United States of America
Corporate Graphics

Table of Contents

4 Map of the West
9 Plants
15 Animals
21 Weather
23 Geography

24 Find Out More
24 Glossary
24 Index
24 About the Author

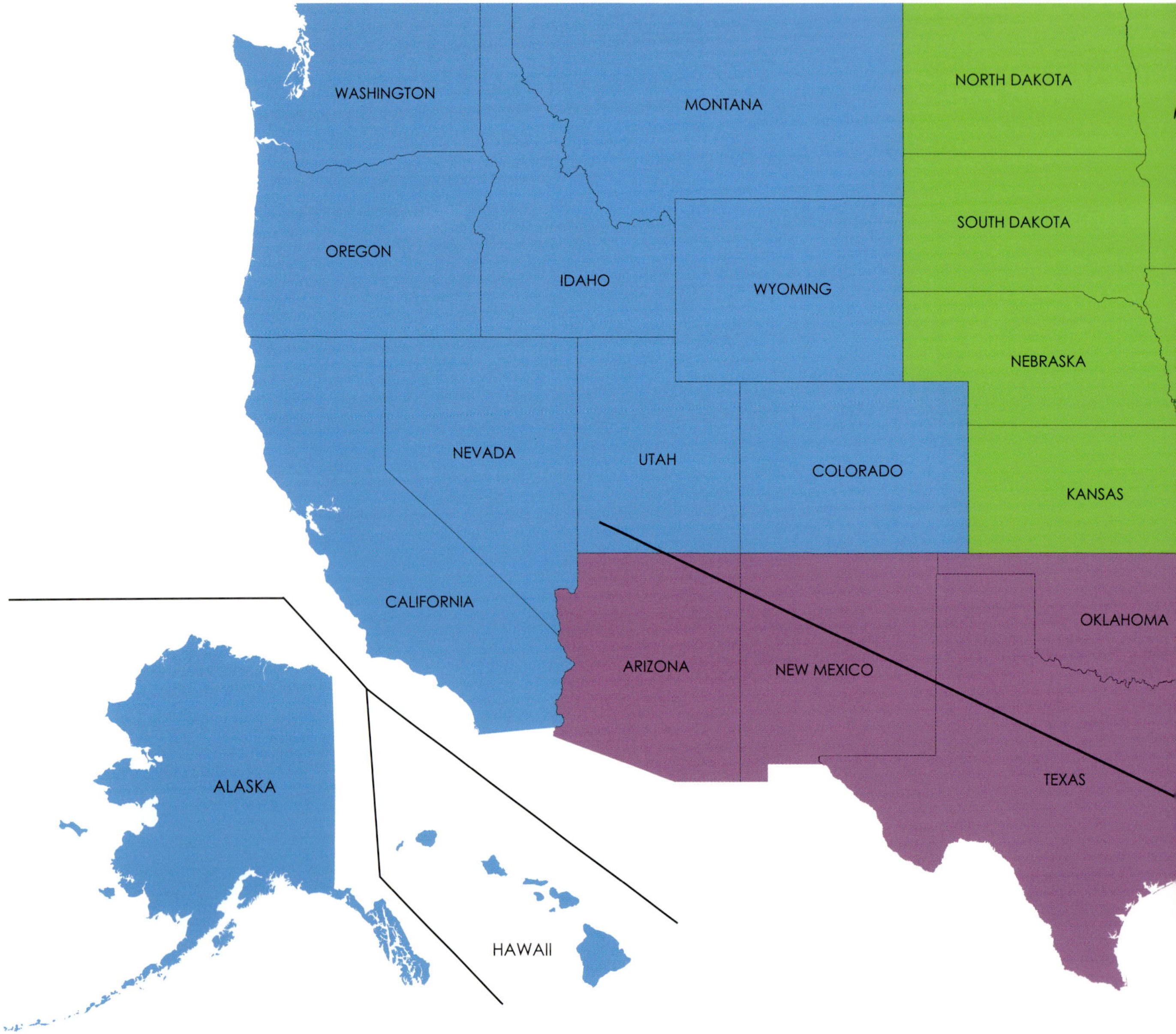
WASHINGTON
MONTANA
NORTH DAKOTA
OREGON
IDAHO
SOUTH DAKOTA
WYOMING
NEBRASKA
NEVADA
UTAH
COLORADO
KANSAS
CALIFORNIA
OKLAHOMA
ARIZONA
NEW MEXICO
ALASKA
TEXAS
HAWAII

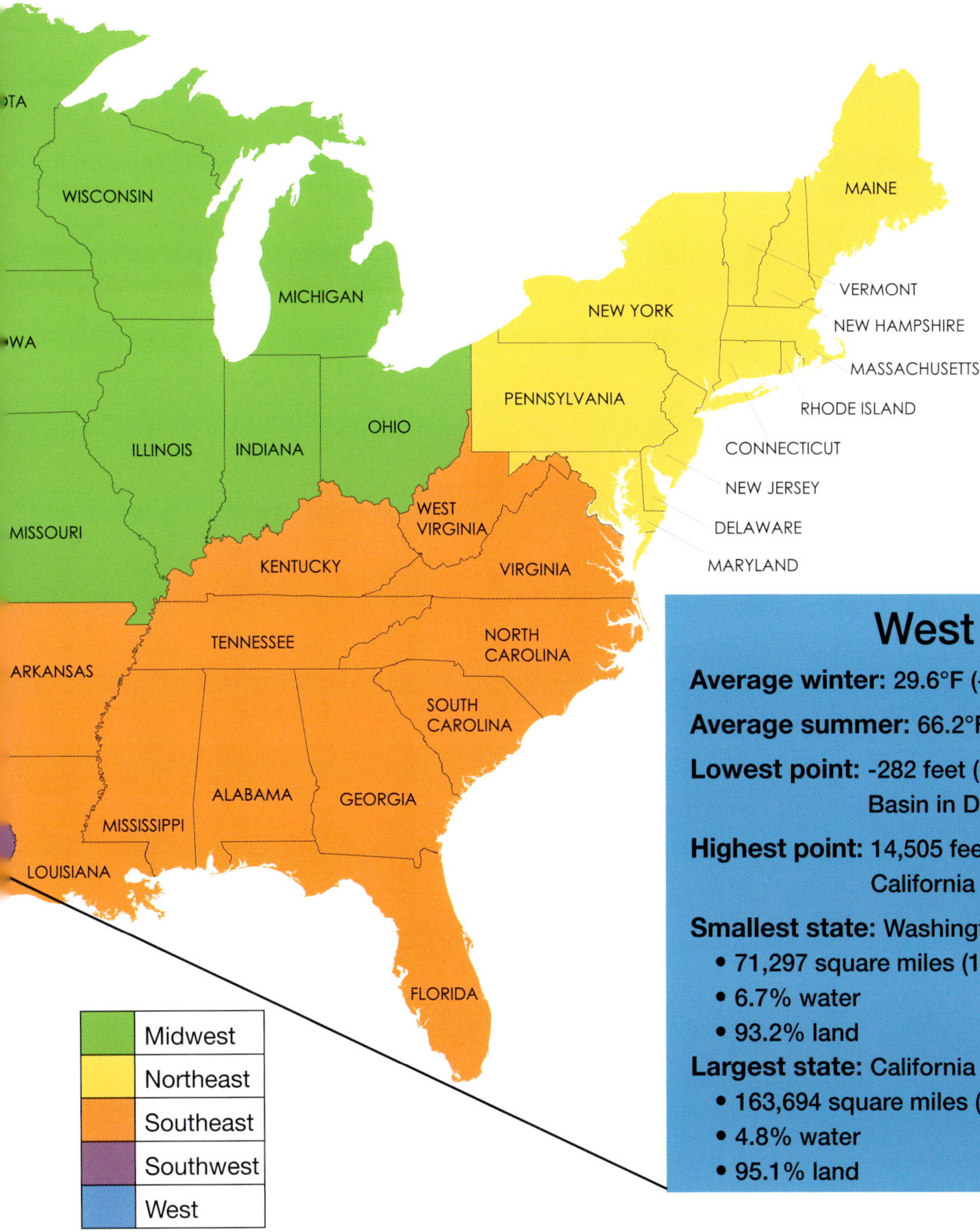

West Facts

Average winter: 29.6°F (-1.3°C)

Average summer: 66.2°F (19°C)

Lowest point: -282 feet (-85.9 m) Badwater Basin in Death Valley, California

Highest point: 14,505 feet (4,421 m) Mount Whitney, California

Smallest state: Washington

- 71,297 square miles (184,658 sq km)
- 6.7% water
- 93.2% land

Largest state: California

- 163,694 square miles (423,965.5 sq km)
- 4.8% water
- 95.1% land

It's time for a nature hike.
Let's see what we can see.

?

What animals do you think eat acorns?

Plants

I see a bee rest on a tiny yellow flower. Now it's flying to a tall plant with pink flowers.

Look at that tall, skinny tree. I think it's a palm tree.

I find an acorn. It's a seed from an oak tree. That's a big seed!

Bitterroot

- Montana's official state flower since 1895.
- This low-growing plant can live over a year without water.

Blueblossom

- This **native** plant of California and Oregon can grow over 10 feet (3 meters) tall.
- The flowers can be used as soap when mixed with water.

Bristlecone Pine Tree

- Nevada's official state tree since 1987.
- The oldest living bristlecone pine is over 5,000 years old.

Coast Rhododendron

- Washington's official state flower since 1959.
- Native to the West Coast, this plant can grow up to 30 feet (9 m) tall.

Oak Tree

- These trees can drink up to 50 gallons (189 liters) of water a day.
- Oak trees start producing acorns after 20 to 50 years.

Oregon Grape Blossom

- Oregon's official state flower since 1899.
- The tiny yellow flowers can be used as **medicine**.

Palm Tree

- There are over 2,500 types of palm trees.
- The California fan palm tree can grow up to 60 feet (18 m) tall.

Redwood Tree

- California's official state tree since 1937.
- The tallest redwood is about 74 feet (22.5 m) taller than the **Statue of Liberty**.

Starfish, or sea stars, only live in oceans. Why do you think this is?

Animals

I hear seagulls. They are so noisy. I see a pelican catch a fish. That bird is quiet.

I found a starfish on my **tide pool** walk. I look but don't touch. Some starfish can be **dangerous**.

American Bison

- Wyoming's official state mammal since 1985.
- This large animal can jump about 6 feet (1.8 m).

Brown Pelican

- This large bird has a bright red throat and long, thin beak.
- Its throat can fill up with over 2 gallons (7.5 L) of water.

Mountain Bluebird

- Official state bird of Idaho and Nevada.
- The female builds the nest while the male pretends to help.

Northern Flying Squirrel

- These common squirrels are nocturnal.
- They "fly" by jumping off a high branch and spreading their front and back legs.

Rocky Mountain Bighorn Sheep

- Colorado's official state animal since 1961.
- Their heavy horns can weigh about 30 pounds (13.6 kilograms).

Rocky Mountain Elk

- Utah's official state animal since 1971.
- A newborn calf, or baby elk, can weigh about 35 pounds (15.8 kg).

Starfish

- These animals have hard, bony skin.
- They can regrow an arm if they lose one.

Western Gull

- These noisy birds are known to steal food.
- They build their nests in colonies, or with other gulls.

Spring

Summer

Fall

Winter

Weather

Sometimes it's wet and foggy during spring. It's hard to see. Other times it's warm and windy.

Summer is almost always sunny. It's hot. I go to the beach and collect seashells.

The air starts to cool again in the fall. The leaves fall to the ground.

I see snow in some places during winter. In other places, I see flowers still in **bloom**.

Beach

Mountain

Forest

Waterfall

Geography

I walk on the beach by the **Pacific Ocean**. I leave footprints in the sand.

I hike up a mountain. Some mountains are bare. Others have trees.

The smell of the forest fills the air. It's dark, but I see sunlight peeking through the leaves.

I see water falling from the top of a hill. The water is moving fast.

Where would you like to hike?

Find Out More

Rau, Dana M. *The West (True Books: U.S. Regions)*. New York: Scholastic, 2012.

Jenson-Elliott, Cynthia L., and Christy Hale. *Antsy Ansel: Ansel Adams, a life in nature*. New York: Christy Ottaviano Books/Henry Holt and Company, 2016.

Glossary

bloom (BLOOM) the flowering state
dangerous (DAYN-jur-uhs) likely to cause harm or injury; not safe
mammal (MAM-uhl) a warm-blooded animal that has hair or fur and usually gives birth to live babies; female mammals produce milk to feed their young
medicine (MED-ih-sin) helpful drugs used to treat illnesses
native (NAY-tiv) an animal or a plant that lives or grows naturally in a certain place
nocturnal (nahk-TUR-nuhl) active at night
Pacific Ocean (puh-SIF-ik OH-shuhn) the world's largest ocean; it borders the western United States
Statue of Liberty (STACH-oo UHV LIB-ur-tee) a monument given to the United States by France as a symbol of peace and freedom; it is located in New York
tide pool (TIDE POOL) an area of water that is left on a beach after the sea level has fallen

Index

beach, 21-23
bird, 15-17, 19
fall, 20-21
flower, 9-12, 21
forest, 22-23
mammal, 16
mountain, 5, 22-23
nocturnal, 17
ocean, 14, 23
spring, 20-21
starfish, 14-15, 19
summer, 5, 20-21
tree, 9, 11-13, 23
waterfall, 22
winter, 5, 20-21

About the Author

Helen Foster James is a volunteer interpretive naturalist for her local state park. She lives by the ocean and loves to hike in the mountains. She is the author of *S Is for S'mores: A Camping Alphabet* and more than 20 other books for children.